HAL LEONARD

GUITARRÓN

BY HERMAN MÉNDEZ

This work is dedicated to my wife, Peggy,
whose encouragement and love have
carried me through life's adventures.

To access video visit:
www.halleonard.com/mylibrary

Enter Code
7305-1711-5047-8264

Cover Photo by: Patrick Nunes
"Parts of the Guitarrón" Photo (page 7) by: Gregory Moore

ISBN 978-1-5400-3132-7

Visit Hal Leonard Online at
www.halleonard.com

Contact us:
Hal Leonard
7777 West Bluemound Road
Milwaukee, WI 53213
Email: info@halleonard.com

In Europe, contact:
Hal Leonard Europe Limited
42 Wigmore Street
Marylebone, London, W1U 2RN
Email: info@halleonardeurope.com

In Australia, contact:
Hal Leonard Australia Pty. Ltd.
4 Lentara Court
Cheltenham, Victoria, 3192 Australia
Email: info@halleonard.com.au

CONTENTS

INTRODUCTION ▶

My first exposure to the deep sound of the guitarrón was at our Mexican family fiestas. There was often a musical group performing mariachi music, and the guitarrón served as the bass voice of the ensemble. The bass sound of the guitarrón was responsible for the frequent shifting between the syncopated and on-beat rhythm of the music.

In recent years, there has been a great interest in music from around the world and a desire by musicians to explore the use of instruments from a variety of cultures to create new sounds, develop new genres of music, and to celebrate the rich music traditions of other people.

The use of this method book will provide the reader with a foundation in the fundamentals of music. The goal is to bridge the gap between playing by ear, which can often be the case with non-traditional western instruments, and playing by reading notated music. Additionally, there is a benefit to standardizing guitarrón performance technique, as it provides for improved performance in the areas of intonation, rhythmic accuracy, and note fingering, for example. Finally, the book can serve to expand the inclusion of the guitarrón's rich bass voice in other genres of music beyond the mariachi by increasing its access to a broader range of musicians.

—Herman Méndez

ABOUT THE VIDEOS

All of the accompanying video lessons and demonstrations for this book can be accessed online for streaming or download. Simply visit *www.halleonard.com/mylibrary* and enter the code found on page 1 of this book. Videos are noted throughout the book with this icon: ▶

PARTS OF THE GUITARRÓN

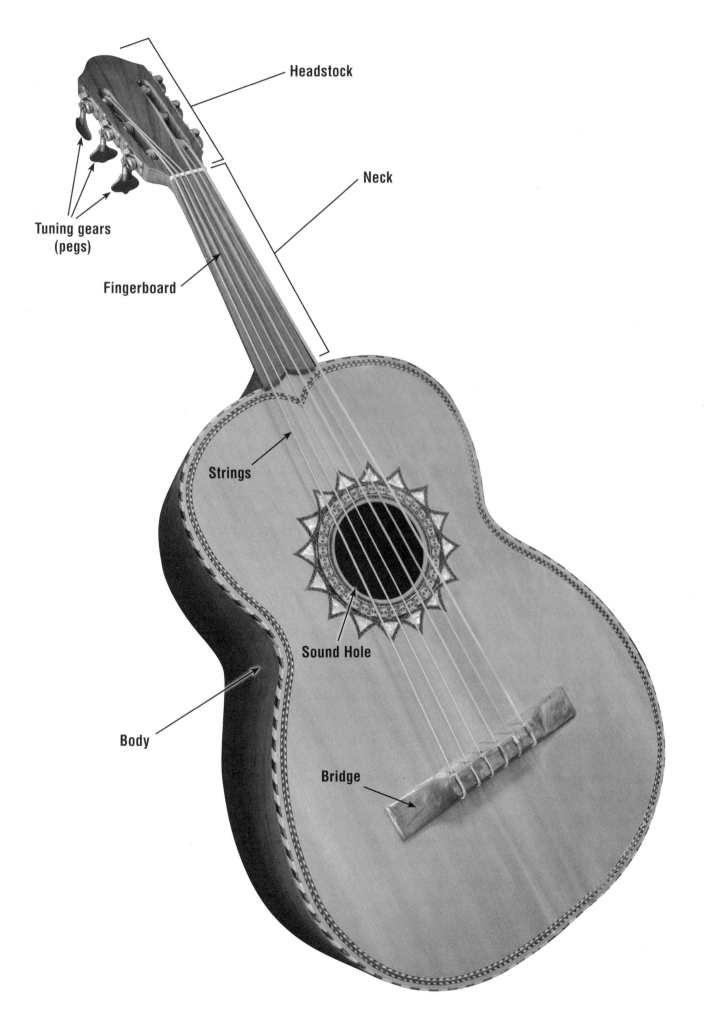

Headstock

Neck

Tuning gears
(pegs)

Fingerboard

Strings

Sound Hole

Body

Bridge

GUITARRÓN TUNING

The strings of the guitarrón are tuned as shown on the piano keyboard and music staff below. Beginning with the lowest or thickest string, the strings are tuned to the following notes: A–D–G–C–E–A. Tuning adjustment is accomplished by turning the tuning gears to loosen or tighten the strings, thereby lowering and raising the pitch of the string, respectively. Caution should be taken to not over-tighten a string, as it can break the string or damage the instrument. It's better to start with a looser string and tighten gradually up to the desired pitch. **Note:** Some guitarróns do not use tuning gears, but instead use tuning pegs to adjust the pitch of each string.

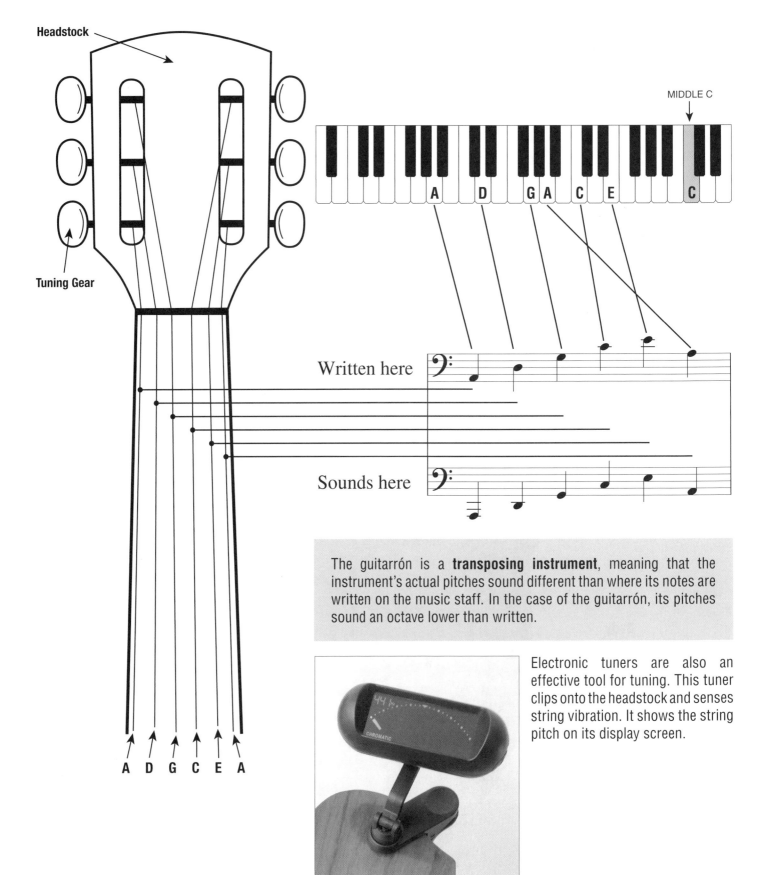

The guitarrón is a **transposing instrument**, meaning that the instrument's actual pitches sound different than where its notes are written on the music staff. In the case of the guitarrón, its pitches sound an octave lower than written.

Electronic tuners are also an effective tool for tuning. This tuner clips onto the headstock and senses string vibration. It shows the string pitch on its display screen.

GUITARRÓN FINGERBOARD

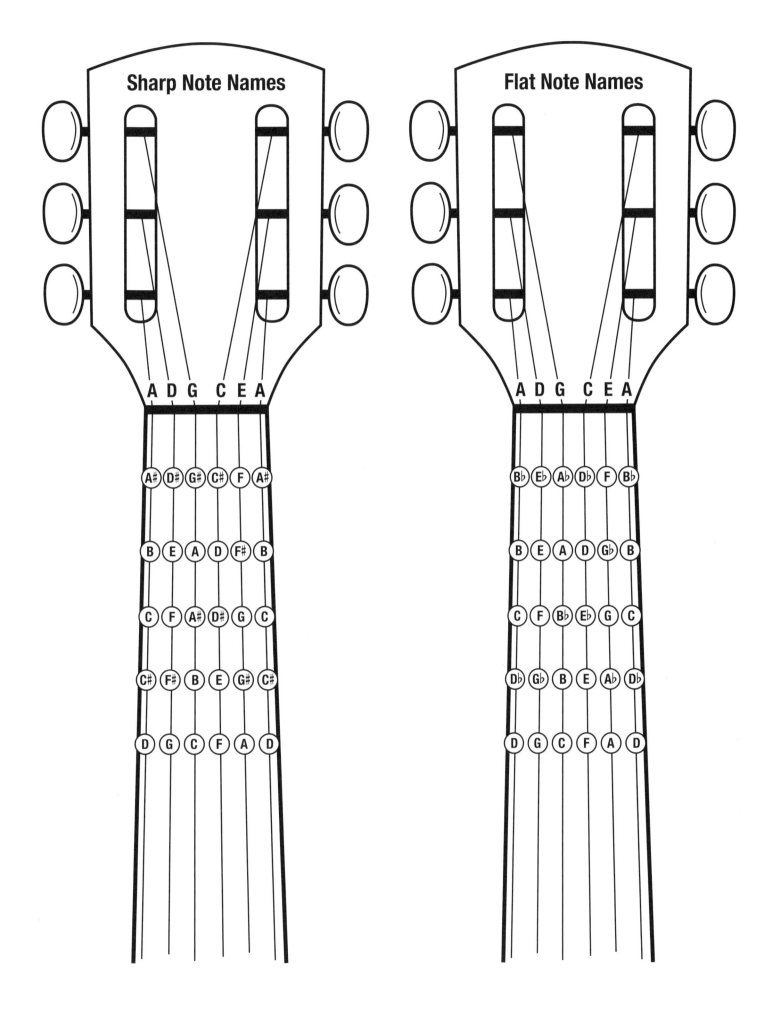

PLAYING THE GUITARRÓN

The notes on the guitarrón can be played individually (one at a time), giving the guitarrón a written range as indicated:

NOTE RANGE

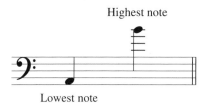

Highest note

Lowest note

Stylistically however (in mariachi music), it is more common that notes are played in octave pairs with what is called a **double stop**; that is to say that the two notes are played simultaneously. Notice below in the written music that, for each of the four beats indicated, there are two notes to be played.

DOUBLE STOPS

Count: 1 2 3 4

On beat 1, there is a low-pitched A and a higher-pitched A (an **octave**, or eight notes, higher). On beat 2, there is a low C and a higher C, and so on.

Notes played in double stops are treated as single notes and therefore are notated using only the lower note for ease of reading and writing.*

Actual notes played   Written notation

*In certain situations, the guitarrónist will be called on to play single notes. These situations may be a result of the performer's personal taste or as desired by the composer—in which it should be explained in the music.

IMPORTANT!

While reading this section, it is recommended that you pause regularly to study the photos and diagrams provided of the hand and finger positions. Note that guitarrón technique is right-hand dominant.

LEFT- AND RIGHT-HAND TECHNIQUE ▶️

The Left Hand

Refer to the photos (starting on page 12) of the left hand, and you will see the positions that the fingers should take when playing the double stop notes. There are 12 hand positions for the 12 double stops that are covered in this book.

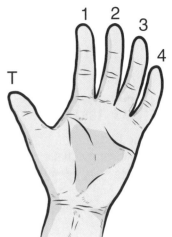

In studying the photos and diagrams, you will notice that the strings are pressed to the fingerboard with various combinations of the fingers and thumb. Pay particular attention to the notes requiring the use of the thumb. The thumb should press the low A string firmly to the fingerboard so that the desired note vibrates clearly and in tune.

When sounding the double stop, you should take care to ensure that you are using the tips of the fingers and that they do not touch any unwanted strings.

The Right Hand

The fingers of the right hand are used to pluck the desired strings, thereby making them vibrate to produce a sound or note. Because the notes are played in pairs, it is necessary to play two strings at the same time. This is done by pinching the strings toward each other, pulling them slightly away from the guitarrón body, and then releasing them.

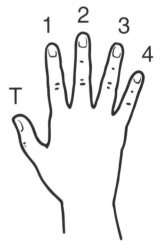

To pluck notes, you will need to develop three techniques:

- **Technique #1:** The thumb (T) and the middle finger (finger 2) will pluck note pairs that use any combination of both outside A strings. The notes that use this technique are A, B♭, B, and C♯.

- **Technique #2:** The thumb (T) and the index finger (finger 1) will be used for all notes that do not use the high A string. The notes that use this technique are: C, D, D♯/E♭, E, F, F♯/G♭, and G.

- **Technique #3:** The thumb alone (T) will be used to play the note G♯. This note is the only one played as a single note.

INITIAL EXERCISES WITH OPEN-STRING NOTES

FIRST NOTE ▶

Unique to guitarrón playing is its use of two simultaneously sounded notes that are an octave apart—i.e., a double stop. The following initial exercises are designed to orient the guitarrónist to the location of the double stops, in which one of the notes is an **open** (or unstopped) string. The reason and benefit of these initial exercises is that they allow the player to compare and adjust the tuning or intonation of the stopped note against the open string, ensuring that both pitches are in tune with each other.

Additionally, each exercise will introduce elements of music notation and music reading. In this manner, the student maximizes instructional practice time by not only learning the notes on the instrument, but also learning music theory fundamentals.

In these initial exercises, the student will find extra notational markings that are meant to aid or support the exercises. These extra markings will not always be included, as later the student will be expected to read more standardized music notation.

Note the following:

- A **fingerboard diagram** is included with the notes. This diagram is similar to the ones used for guitar except that:

  1. There are no frets/lines on the guitarrón, and therefore the lines in the diagrams are indicated only to show relative note positions.

  2. Unlike for the guitar, in which the diagrams are used for chords, the guitarrón diagrams show the single or octave-paired notes.

  3. The diagram, along with the photos of the left hand, will help you use the correct fingers as well as find the location of the desired note(s) on the fingerboard.

- At the bottom of each staff of music you will also find a "count" to aid in counting the value of each note.

- Right-hand fingerings are also indicated and match the finger numbers on the drawing of the right hand shown on page 11. Specifically, T = thumb, 1 = index finger, and 2 = middle finger.

EXERCISES ON C

The first exercises you will play use the open (or unstopped) C string and the stopped low C note, which is located on the low A string.

To play the low C, stroke the string with the thumb (T) of the right hand using a motion that pulls the string away from the instrument. The right hand will also move, along with the thumb, in a direction away from the body of the guitarrón.

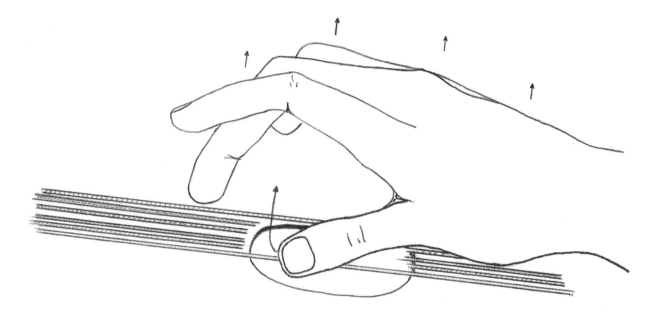

To play the high C string, use the index finger (1) to pluck the string away from the body of the instrument. Here again, the right hand moves away from the guitarrón, along with the finger.

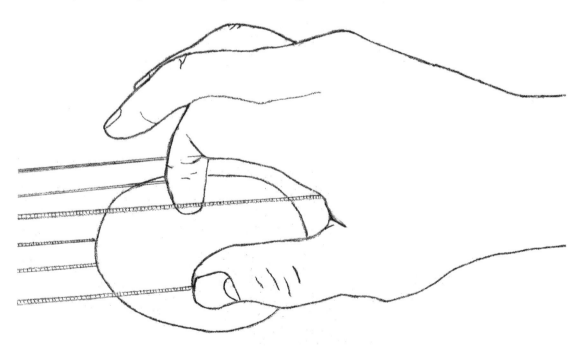

When you play the high C and low C notes at the same time, you get a double stop.

Exercises 1, 2, and 3 introduce the note C as a single note and as an octave pair or double stop. You will notice that the high C is an open string, so if your instrument is properly tuned, you will only need to concern yourself with the intonation of the lower C.

To play the low C, you will press the string to the fingerboard with the thumb of the left hand (refer to the hand position photos on page 12). As you play, adjust your thumb by sliding it up or down the length of the A string so that the low C is in tune with the high (open) C.

STAFF BASICS

Music for the guitarrón is written on a staff using the **bass clef**. The names of the notes are determined by the **space** or **line** on which they are written. Notes above or below the staff are written on **ledger lines**. The lines and spaces of the bass clef are assigned the following notes:

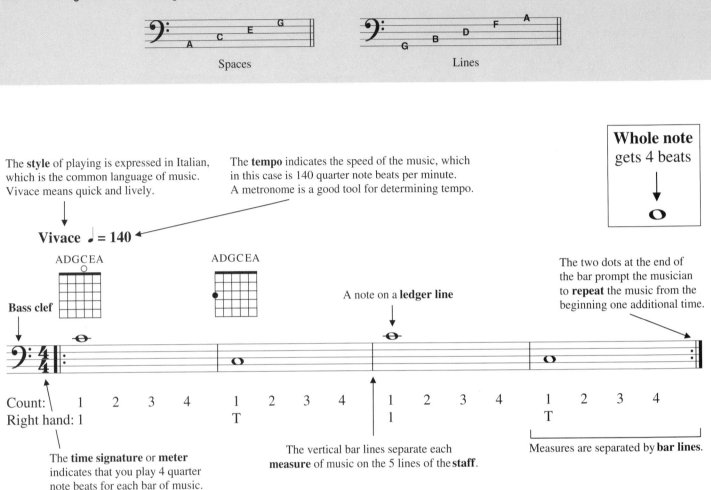

For more music basics, refer to the Music Fundamentals section of this book.

EXERCISE 1

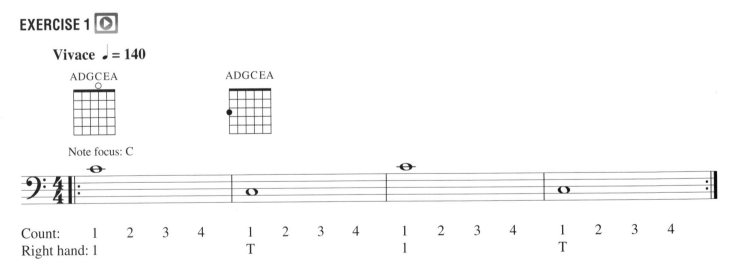

In the second and third exercises, you will now add the double stop for the note C. To play the low C and the high C simultaneously, as in the second bar of Exercise 2 and all of Exercise 3, the thumb and the index finger pluck both strings at the same time in a pinching motion.

EXERCISE 2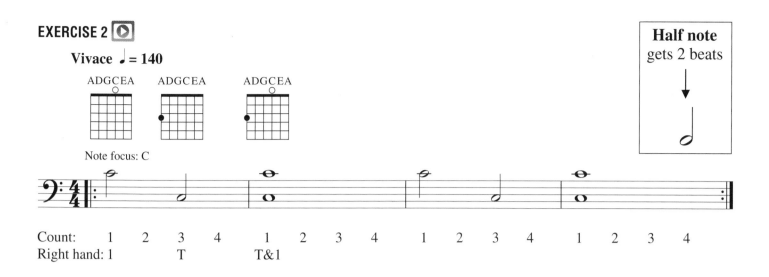

Vivace ♩ = 140

ADGCEA ADGCEA ADGCEA

Note focus: C

Count:	1	2	3	4	1	2	3	4	1	2	3	4	1	2	3	4
Right hand:	1		T		T&1											

Half note
gets 2 beats

EXERCISE 3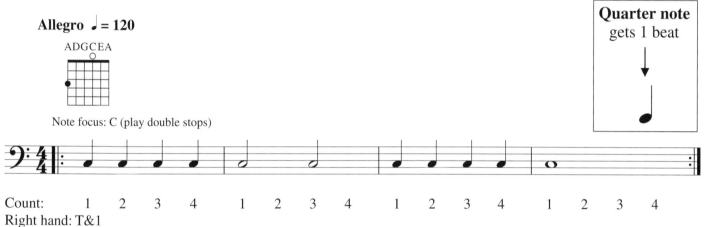
Remember to play double stops for each note, even though only the lower-pitched note is written!

Allegro ♩ = 120

ADGCEA

Note focus: C (play double stops)

Count:	1	2	3	4	1	2	3	4	1	2	3	4	1	2	3	4
Right hand:	T&1															

Quarter note
gets 1 beat

EXERCISES ON D

As with the previous exercises, adjust the pitch of the stopped note to the open-string note by sliding the second finger of the left hand along the length of the string. Tune the high D pitch to match the low D, so that they are an octave apart.

Reminder: Refer to the photos of the hand and finger positions to help in identifying the correct hand and finger placements.

EXERCISE 4

Vivace ♩ = 140

ADGCEA

ADGCEA

Note focus: D

Key signature indicates the sharp and flat notes

Count:	1	2	3	4	1	2	3	4	etc.
Right hand:	T				1				

ADGCEA

Count:	1	2	3	4	1	2	3	4	1	2	3	4	1	2	3	4
Right hand:	T		1						T&1							

EXERCISE 5

Vivace ♩ = 140

ADGCEA

Note focus: D (play double stops)

Count:	1	2	3	4	1	2	3	4	1	2	3	4	1	2	3	4
Right hand:	T&1															

MUTING

The technique of **muting** (to silence or dampen a string or strings) is useful and necessary for situations like changing notes, encountering rests, the end of a music selection, and/or if the style of the music calls for it.

Muting can be accomplished by resting the side of the right hand, opposite the thumb, on the string(s) between the sound hole and the bridge of the guitarrón. This type of muting works well at the end of a piece of music.

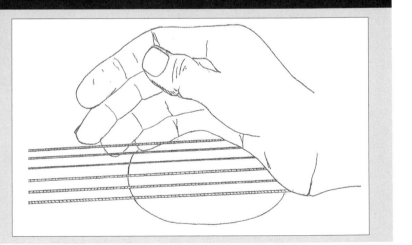

Another muting technique involves the use of the left hand. Just before a new note is sounded, the underside of the fingers and thumb reach across the fingerboard and touch the strings to keep them from sounding (as if to close the grip around the neck of the guitarrón). The hand maintains the position from the note(s) just played, and the strings are not pressed to the fingerboard. Instead, they're touched with enough pressure to quickly stop the sound and prepare for the next note or rest. This type of muting can be used appropriately during a piece of music.

It is also possible to mute notes by simply releasing the pressure of the left-hand fingers so that the strings are no longer touching the fingerboard. The fingers will still need to remain in contact with the strings to keep them from vibrating, but they should not be pressing the strings down to the fingerboard.

Practice the various muting techniques in Exercises 6 and 7, keeping in mind that you can use one technique or a combination of techniques to achieve the desired effect. You should also experiment to find other methods not presented in this book. In any case, practice slowly and deliberately, increasing the speed of the exercises as you become more comfortable with string muting.

Note: In the exercises that introduce a new octave pair, muting is not a concern because you want to continue hearing the note that you just sounded along with the current note (this allows you to compare the intonation between notes).

EXERCISES ON C AND D

In Exercises 6 and 7, the notes C and D are both played as double stops. Keep in mind that, even though you are playing a pair of notes (double stops), only the lower note is written.

Notice that the half rest ( ) is introduced in Exercise 6 at measure 5. The **half rest** represents two beats of silence, which is obtained by muting or silencing the strings. Also notice that the time signature is now indicated by a "C," which stands for "common time." This is simply another manner of representing a 4/4 meter. The use of the **natural symbol** (♮) on the note C cancels the C♯ indicated in the key signature for measures 2, 3, 6, and 7.

EXERCISE 6

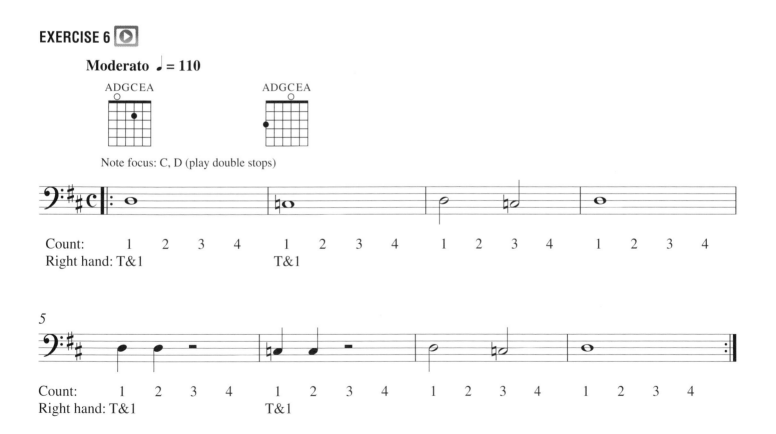

Allegro ♩ = 130

Note focus: C, D (play double stops)

Count: 1   2   3   4   1   2   3   4   1   2   3   4   1   2   3   4

Right hand: T&1   T&1

5

9

13

Allegro ♩ = 130

Note focus: C, D (play double stops)

Count: 1   2   3   4   1   2   3   4   1   2   3   4   1   2   3   4

Right hand: T&1   T&1

5

EXERCISES ON E

The waltz and "el son" (Spanish) are two styles of music that are in 3/4 time. The waltz is European in origin, while "el son" is typically associated with Mexican mariachi music. Johann Strauss's "The Blue Danube" is a famous waltz, while a well-known son is "El Son de la Negra."

Exercises 9 and 10, while not necessarily waltzes or sones, are nonetheless in 3/4 meter. This simply means there are three beats for each measure of music. Notice the dotted half note in measures 4 and 8. A **dot** extends a note's duration by one half of its value. Therefore, whereas a **half note** lasts for two beats, a **dotted half note** lasts for three beats.

EXERCISE 9

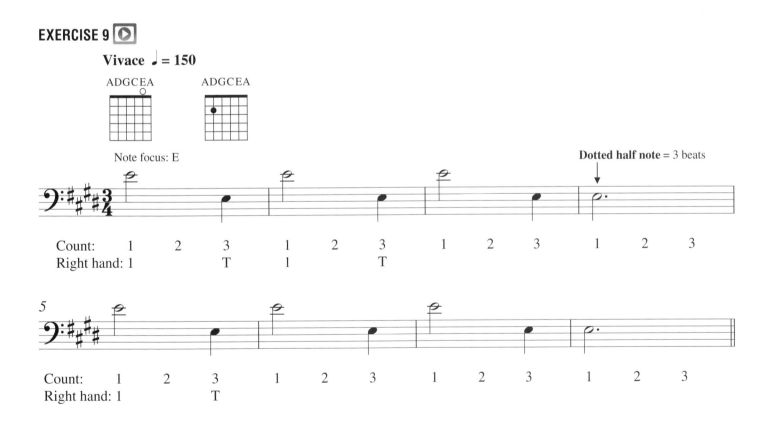

EXERCISE 10

EXERCISES ON C, D, AND E

Here are some easy melodies to play using the first three notes you've learned.

HOT CROSS BUNS

Traditional English Folk Song

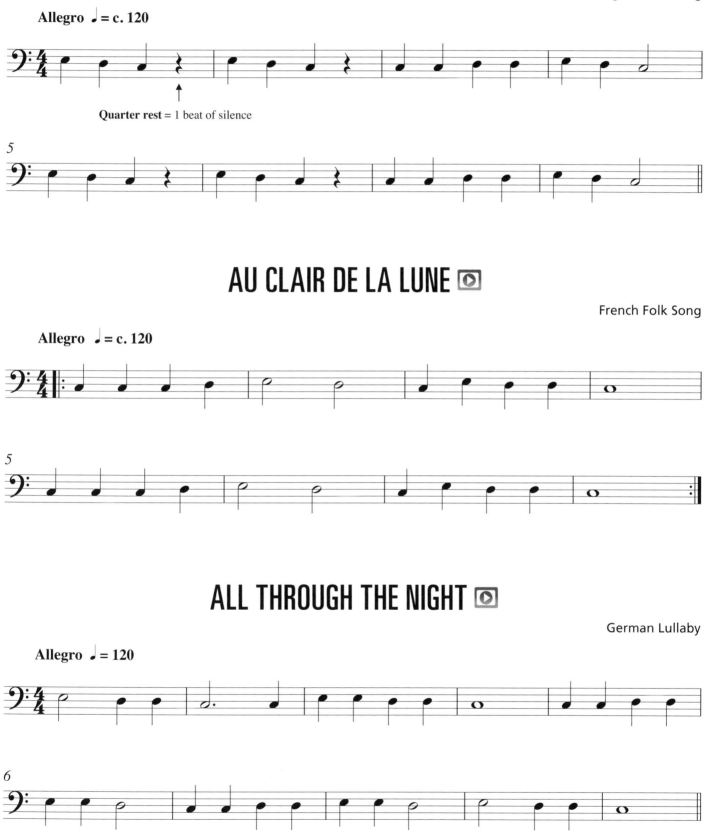

AU CLAIR DE LA LUNE

French Folk Song

ALL THROUGH THE NIGHT

German Lullaby

EXERCISES ON A

The exercises for the A note use the two open outer strings: the low-pitched A and the high-pitched A.

To play the low A, stroke the string with the thumb (T) of the right hand using a motion that pulls the string away from the instrument. The right hand will also move, along with the thumb, in a direction away from the body of the guitarrón.

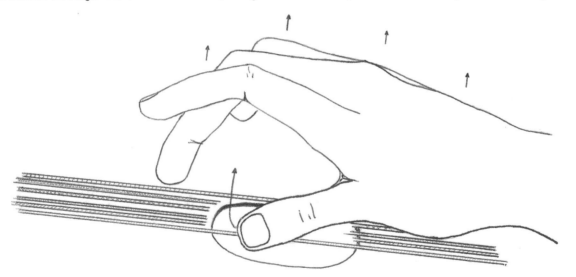

To play the high A string, use the middle finger (2) to pull the string away from the body of the instrument. Here again, the right hand moves away from the guitarrón, along with the finger.

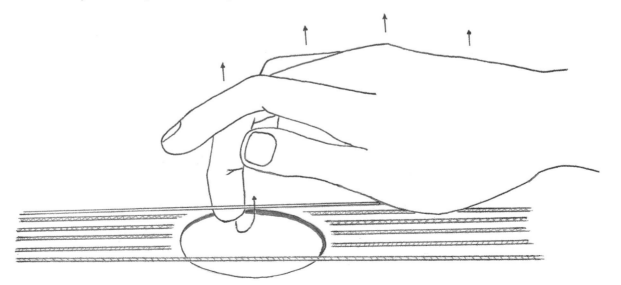

Exercise 12 is played in a 2/4 meter. There are two beats for each measure of music.

EXERCISE 12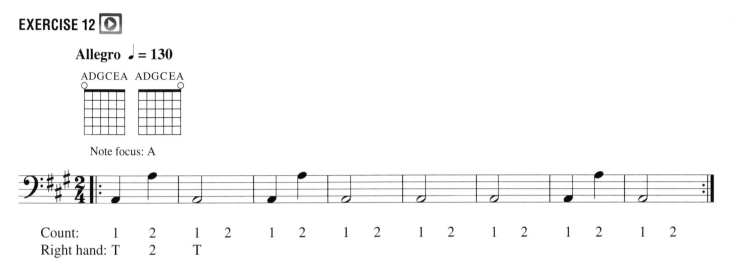

The **eighth note** is introduced in Exercise 13. An eighth note is twice as fast as a quarter note; i.e., there are two eighth notes in each beat. To get a feel for the subdivision of the beat, it's helpful to clap a steady beat and say a two-syllable word for each beat.

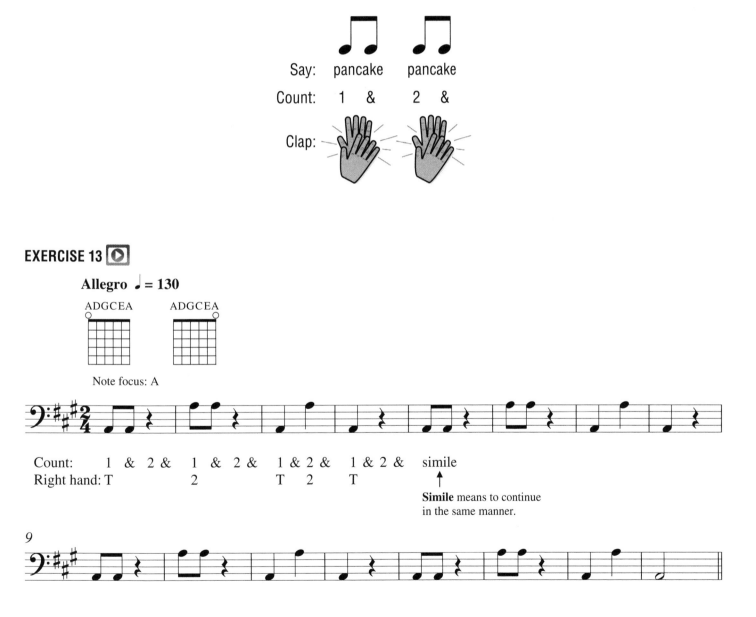

EXERCISE 13

Simile means to continue in the same manner.

To play the low A and the high A simultaneously (as in Exercises 14 and 15), the thumb and the middle finger pluck both strings at the same time in a pinching motion.

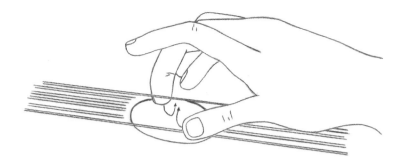

SYNCOPATION

Syncopation is an offset of the main beat by placing an emphasis on what is normally a weak beat. In Exercise 14, we see an example of syncopation in measures 1, 2, 5, and 6. In this exercise, the beat is offset by an **eighth rest** (silence for the duration of an eighth note, or half of a beat). Exercise 15 also provides an example of a syncopated rhythm in measures 8 and 10.

Note the **dotted quarter notes**. Whereas a quarter note lasts for one beat, a dotted quarter note lasts for one and a half beats.

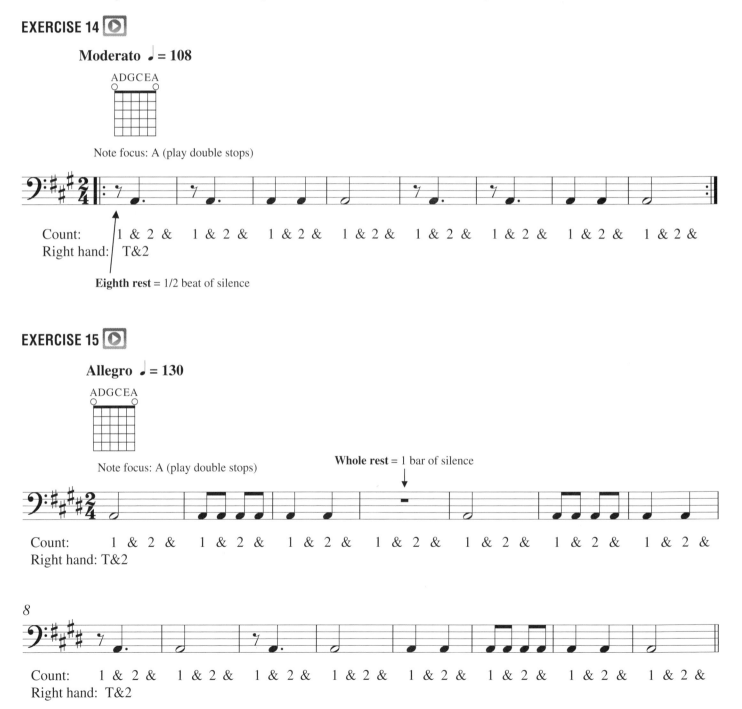

24

ACCOMPANIMENT

Bass instruments serve the important role of providing accompaniment in a music ensemble. This means they help create the pulse and define the harmony and style of the music. Here are three examples of typical bass parts.

POLKA

Rhythmically, the **polka** is a quick dance style in **duple meter** such as 2/4 or **cut time**, which provides a two-beat pulse for every measure. This example uses cut time, which means that the time values of all the notes and rests are cut in half, and each measure is counted as two beats instead of four.

POLKA ACCOMPANIMENT

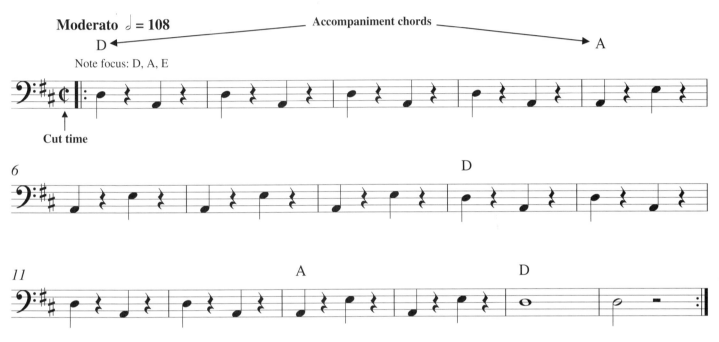

WALTZ

The **waltz** is another dance style played in the **triple meter** of 3/4. Stylistically, the bass instrument plays on the first beat of each bar, with other instruments playing chords on the second and third beats of each bar.

WALTZ ACCOMPANIMENT

POP ROCK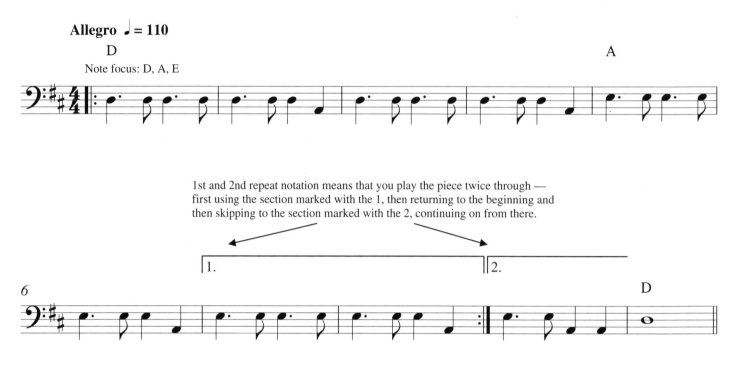

This next pattern works well with a variety of songs that require a steady pulse, as is found in many popular and contemporary songs. The dotted quarter note and eighth note pattern provides a rhythm that moves the music in a forward feel. Experiment playing the pattern at different speeds, as it works well with slow, medium, and fast tempos.

POP ROCK ACCOMPANIMENT

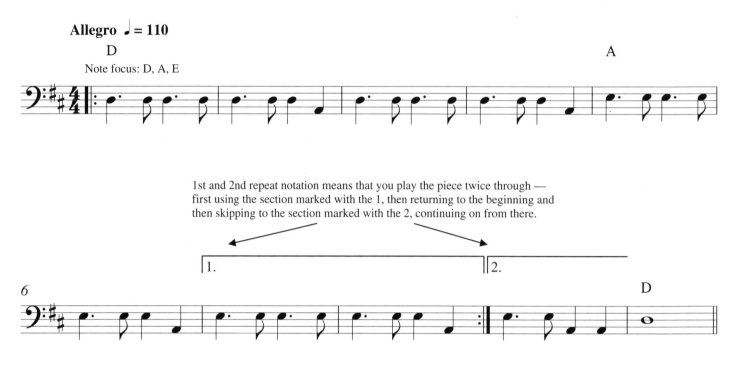

1st and 2nd repeat notation means that you play the piece twice through — first using the section marked with the 1, then returning to the beginning and then skipping to the section marked with the 2, continuing on from there.

ACCOMPANIMENT NOTE SELECTION

You likely observed that the previous three accompaniment examples all used the same three notes of D, A, and E to define a harmonic progression. Music progresses or has a sense of direction by way of the harmonic structure that supports a melody. The harmonic structure can be expressed in the form of chords, which are commonly played by chordal instruments, such as guitar or piano. The most basic chord, a **triad**, uses a combination of three tones sounded together.

Our three examples employed two chords, both of which are built on a D major scale. The D major chord (represented by the **chord symbol** "D") is created by using the first (D), third (F#), and fifth (A) notes of the D major scale (refer to the scale that follows). This first chord in a key is called the **tonic** chord. The other chord in the examples was an A major chord, and it's built with the fifth (A), seventh (C#), and second (E) tones of the D major scale. This chord is called the **dominant** chord.

Bass accompaniment, which is also referred to as a **bass line**, relies primarily on the use of the first note (**root** note) and fifth note of a chord. So, for a D major chord, our bass line uses the notes D and A; for the A chord, our bass line uses the A and E notes.

The root and 5th provide for the strongest harmonic support and happen on the strongest beats of the music. In all three of our examples, the 3rd of the chord is not utilized.

Also, just as the root and 5th of a chord provide the strongest harmonic chord definition within any given chord, so too do the chords built on the first scale degree (the tonic) and fifth scale degree (the dominant) provide for the strongest harmonic progression within the overall key of most music.

In summary, for much contemporary and traditional music, the bass instrument's most important notes are the root and 5th of a chord, and the most common triad chords in a piece of music are those constructed on the first (tonic) and fifth (dominant) scale degree of a key. The example below illustrates these fundamental ideas for the key of D major, which can be applied to other keys and chords as well.

KEY OF D MAJOR – D MAJOR AND A MAJOR CHORDS

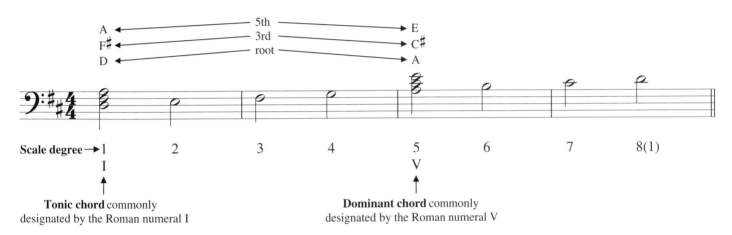

MORE EXERCISES WITH OPEN-STRING NOTES

EXERCISES ON G

Important: While first practicing the exercises, do not worry about playing the music exactly as written (that will be the eventual goal). More specifically and strictly speaking, after playing a note, it needs to stop sounding before the next note is played. But for now, allow the notes to sound longer than written and to overlap with the note that follows. The reason for this is that it lets you hear and compare the intonation of the stopped note to the open-string note. Use the preceding suggestion with all the exercises that include an open string. As you become comfortable in knowing that you are playing in tune, you can mute notes as needed to play the music as written.

EXERCISE 16

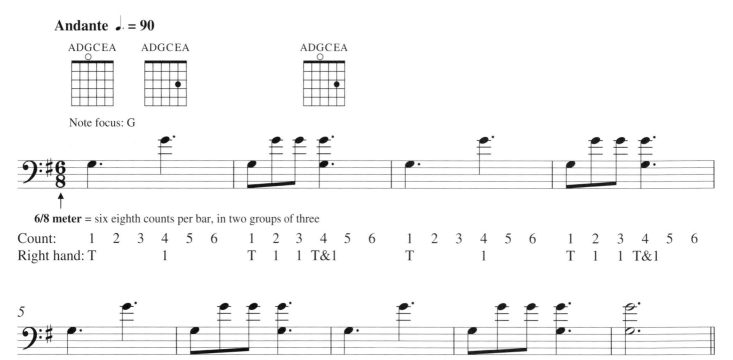

6/8 meter = six eighth counts per bar, in two groups of three

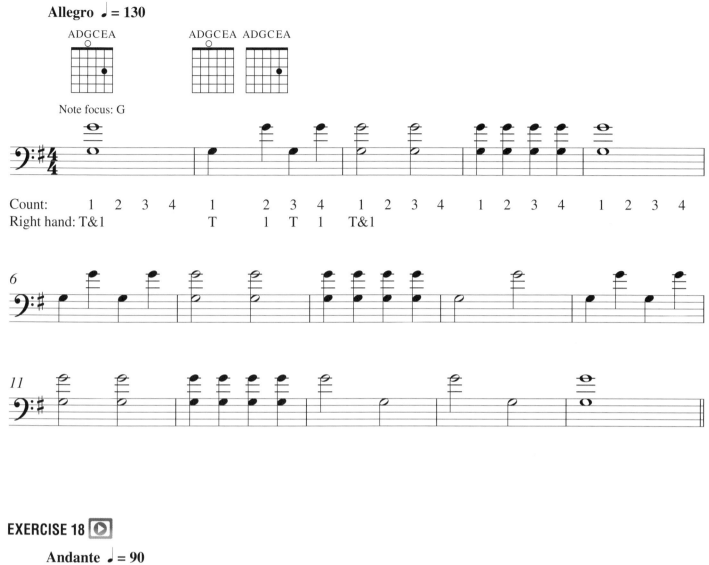

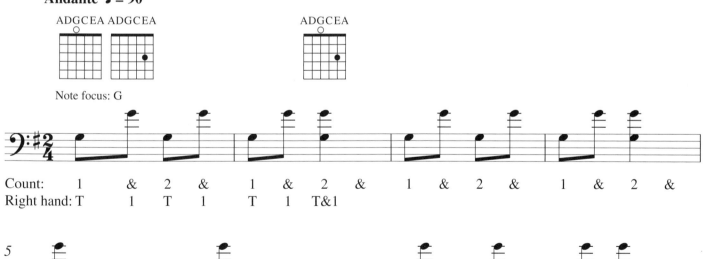

EXERCISES ON C, D, E, A, AND G

EXERCISE 19

LA CUCARACHA

Traditional Mexican Folk Song

31

EXERCISES USING ONLY STOPPED NOTES

Beginning with Exercise 21, the remaining notes to be learned are introduced as double stops and not as single notes. If desired, the student can create their own exercises—or adapt the initial exercises with these remaining notes—to practice the intonation between the high and the low pitches, as was modeled in the open-string exercises.

ENHARMONIC NOTES

In general, **enharmonic notes** are tones that sound identical though they are named differently. The name of the note is changed depending on the key of the music or the particular musical phrase. In the key of G major, for example, the seventh note of the scale is F#, while that same note is called G♭ in the key of D♭ major. Some other examples of enharmonic tones include C#/D♭, E#/F, etc. (refer to the scales section of this book). In the following exercises, you will encounter enharmonic notes.

EXERCISES ON F

Exercise 21 introduces the note F, and it's played along with the notes A, C, and G, which were covered in the initial exercises. The F does not use an open string and therefore care should be used to ensure that both the low and the high F are in tune—both to each other and in relation to the other notes.

Practice the exercise slowly and work up to the speed indicated. Singing the pitches as you play them can be a great aid to hearing and playing in tune.

EXERCISE 21

Andante ♩ = 115

ADGCEA

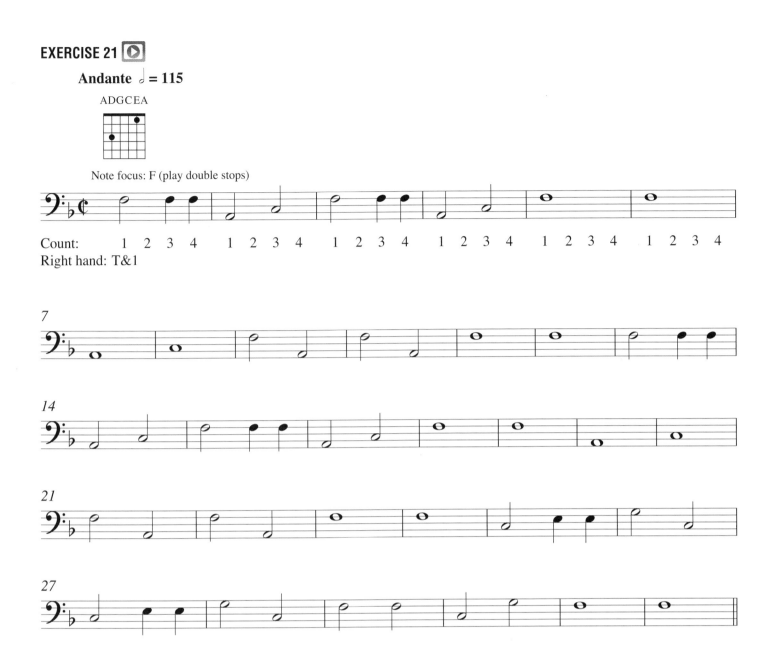

Note focus: F (play double stops)

Count: 1 2 3 4 1 2 3 4 1 2 3 4 1 2 3 4 1 2 3 4 1 2 3 4
Right hand: T&1

Familiarity with Beethoven's "Ode to Joy" will also afford you the opportunity to hear and play the F in tune within the context of this well-known melody.

ODE TO JOY

Ludwig van Beethoven

Allegro ♩ = c. 120

ACCIDENTALS

Notes that are not part of the scale or key of a piece of music are referred to as **accidentals**. Exercise 22 uses an A natural in the key of B major, and in Exercise 23, we see the use of a B natural in the key of B♭ major. Neither of these notes are part of the key signature in their respective exercises.

These accidentals are sometimes called **chromatic alterations** and are added or cancelled through the use of five different signs:

- (♯) A **sharp** raises the pitch by a **half step** (the smallest distance between two notes; the distance from one piano key to the very next adjacent key is a half step).

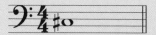

- (♭) A **flat** lowers the pitch by a half step.

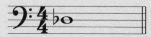

- (𝄪) A **double sharp** raises the pitch by two half steps.

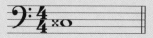

- (♭♭) A **double flat** lowers the pitch by two half steps.

- (♮) A **natural** cancels a previous accidental or instructs you to play a natural version of a note that would normally be played sharp or flat, according to the key signature.

Accidentals are only in effect for the specific bar in which they are indicated.

EXERCISES ON B

Exercise 22 uses a syncopated rhythmic pattern. The A natural provides an opportunity to check the intonation of the B against the open string A.

EXERCISE 22

In the following folk song, we see the use of a **tie**. This curved line connecting two (or more) notes combines the rhythmic value of both notes. In other words, you pluck the first note and sustain it through the duration of the tied note as well, without plucking it again.

CIELITO LINDO

Traditional Mexican Folk Song

EXERCISES ON A#/Bb

Exercise 23 provides an example of a **chromatic** line of notes, which are notes moving by half steps: A–Bb–B–C.

EXERCISE 23

LAS CHIAPANECAS

Traditional Mexican Folk Song

EXERCISES ON D#/Eb

A D G C E A

Left hand

Right hand → T   1

EXERCISE 24

Vivace ♩ = 125

ADGCEA

Note focus: Eb (play double stops)

Count: 1   2   3   4   1   2   3   4   1   2   3   4   1   2   3   4   1   2   3   4

Right hand: T&1

EXERCISE 25

Andante ♩. = 90

ADGCEA

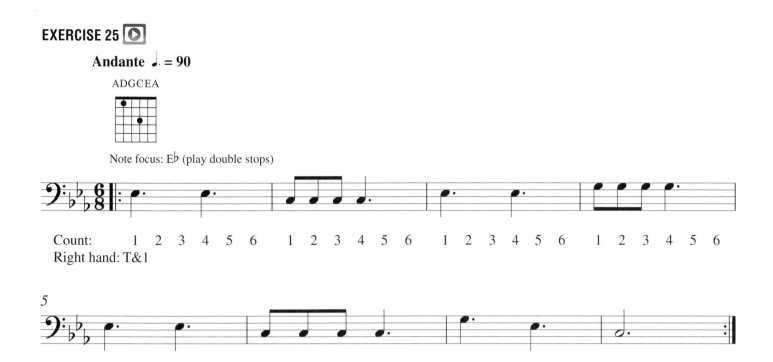

Note focus: E♭ (play double stops)

Count: 1   2   3   4   5   6   1   2   3   4   5   6   1   2   3   4   5   6   1   2   3   4   5   6

Right hand: T&1

WHEN THE SAINTS GO MARCHING IN

New Orleans Processional

Allegro ♩ = 100

EXERCISES ON F♯/G♭

Note: Be prepared to play the F♯ accidental, beginning in bar 11. Before you play the exercise, identify the note in the music, locate and position your fingers on the instrument for the note, and pluck the note a couple of times with the goal of playing in tune and with good tone.

EXERCISE 26 ▶

LAS MAÑANITAS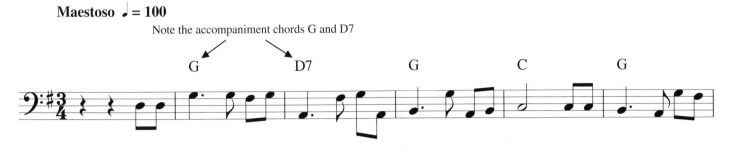

Traditional Mexican Folk Song

AURA LEE

Traditional American

EXERCISES ON C#/Db

EXERCISE 27 ▶

Vivace ♩ = 120

ADGCEA

Note focus: C# (play double stops)

Count: 1 2 3 4   1 2 3 4   1 2 3 4   1 2 3 4   1 2 3 4
Right hand: T&2

6

12

EXERCISE 28 ▶

Moderato ♩ = 120

ADGCEA

Note focus: Db (play double stops)

LONG, LONG AGO

Thomas Haynes Bayly

AMERICA

Traditional

EXERCISES ON G#/A♭

In Exercises 29 and 30, the A♭/G# note comprises the lower note of what would be the double stop, but because the higher A♭/G# is not easily reached by the fingers of the left hand, it is not played. Therefore, you'll play it as a single note.

EXERCISE 29 ▶

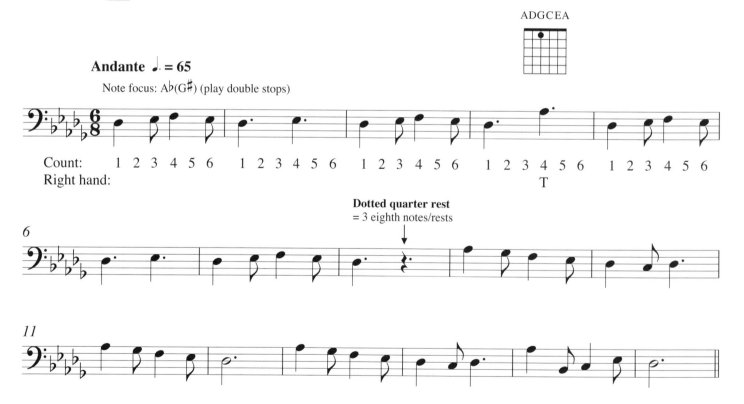

44

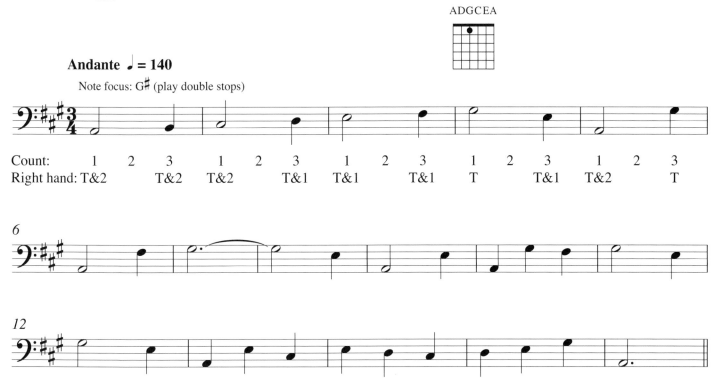

THEME FROM FIRST SYMPHONY

Johannes Brahms

THE CIRCLE OF FIFTHS

The **circle of fifths** is a series of tonal relationships that connect major and minor keys. Basically, if you start on any given note and travel by moving in 5ths from note to note, you will eventually return to the note on which you began (refer to the diagrams below).

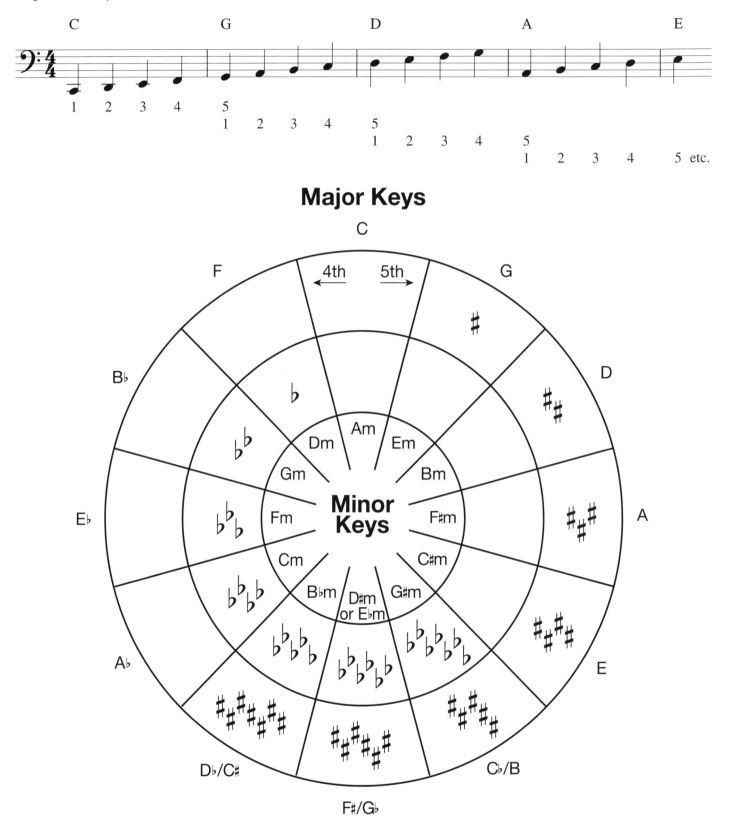

Many songs and compositions use the harmonic relationships shown in the circle of fifths. If you play the cycle many times, your ear will eventually grow accustomed to the harmonic sequence, and you will develop a natural instinct for moving through the cycle when the song you are playing uses a part of it.

Following are two exercises—one for major triads and one for minor triads—that progress through the circle of fifths. These two exercises are great for daily practice because they involve reading and playing all the 12 tones and hand positions found in this book.

CIRCLE OF FIFTHS – MAJOR TRIADS

CIRCLE OF FIFTHS – MINOR TRIADS

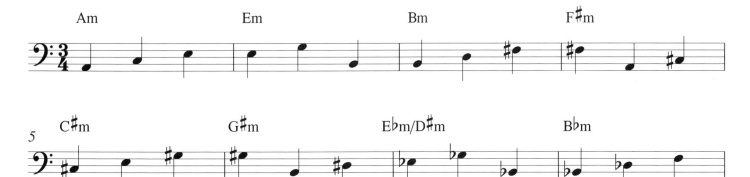

The major and relative natural minor scales have the same key signature. The natural minor begins on the sixth note of the major scale.

FREQUENTLY USED SCALES

LESS FREQUENTLY USED SCALES

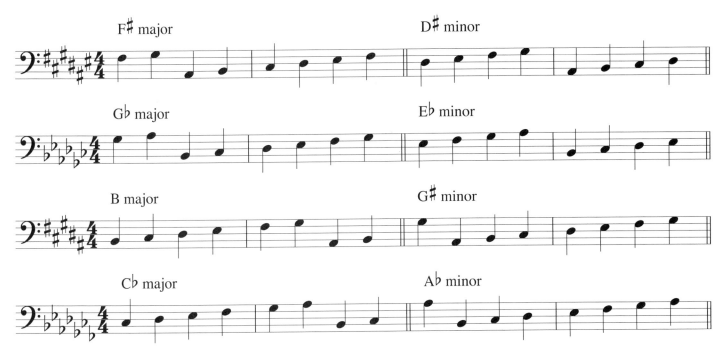

MUSIC FUNDAMENTALS

THE GREAT STAFF

Western music is commonly written on a series of lines and spaces that form what is called the **great staff** (or **grand staff**). The great staff is divided into two staves: the treble staff (for high-pitched sounds) and the bass staff (for low-pitched sounds).

Treble staff

Bass staff

Ledger lines are added when notes are higher or lower than either staff can accommodate.

Staff {   Ledger lines

THE BASS STAFF

Since the guitarrón is a low-pitched instrument, its notes are written on the bass staff.

This is the **bass clef** sign:

The names of the notes are determined by the space or line on which they are written.

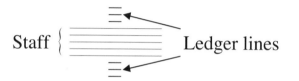

Spaces   Lines

Using the first letter of each space or line to form a sentence or phrase can help you recall the names of the lines and spaces.

Spaces: All **C**ows **E**at **G**rass

Lines: Good **B**oys **D**o **F**ine **A**lways

NOTE AND REST VALUES

A note has two basic elements: its **pitch** (how high or low it is) and its **rhythmic duration** (how long the sound or silence lasts). A rest also has a rhythmic duration and is in effect the opposite of a note. In other words, a note indicates sound, while a rest indicates silence. Through the various combinations of notes and rests, the basics of music can be written down or notated so that it can later be performed as audible music.

Below are the various notes and rests found in written music:

1 whole note/rest equals

2 half notes/rests or

4 quarter notes/rests or

8 eighth notes/rests or

16 sixteenth notes/rests or

32 thirty-second notes/rests

Note Value Relationships

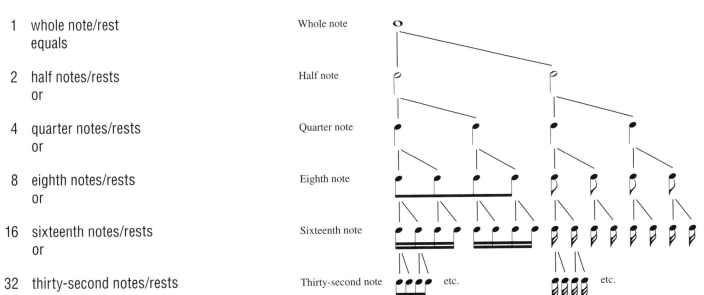

Rest Value Relationships

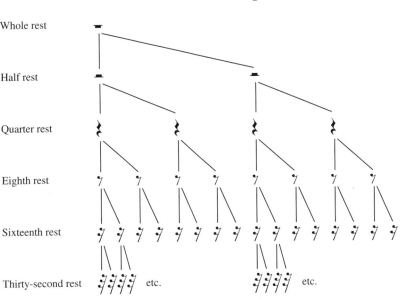

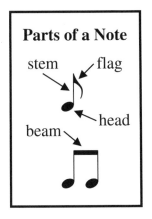

Parts of a Note

stem — flag

beam — head

TIME SIGNATURES

Music is grouped into beats or counts that are placed into what is called a **measure** (or **bar**). The first beat of a measure is normally accented or emphasized. Measures of music are separated by **bar lines**.

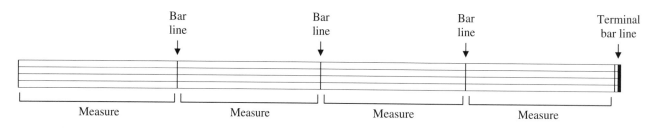

Note: The **terminal bar line** at the end indicates the end of the music. Sometimes a double (thin) bar line is used at the end of a music section or excerpt.

A measure contains a limited number of **beats**. The number of beats in a measure is indicated by the **time signature** (or **meter**), which consists of two numbers. The bottom number indicates what note value is to be used as the basic beat or pulse, while the upper number indicates how many of those types of notes will fit into each measure of music.

This time signature is 2/4. There are two beats to a measure, with each beat having a value of a quarter note.

This time signature is 6/8. In this meter, there will be six eighth notes in each measure of music.

Note that a time signature can also be indicated with a letter "C." The C stands for "common time" and is the same as a time signature of 4/4 (four quarter notes per measure).

TEMPO

It should be mentioned that the time signature does not describe how fast or slow a piece of music is to be played. The speed or **tempo** of a piece of music is indicated at the beginning of the written music and be can be indicated as a number (**beats per minute**, or **bpm**) or a descriptive word or phrase.

In the following example, the tempo is written at the upper left-hand corner of the staff. We also see that the time signature is 2/4, or two quarter notes to a bar of music.

The tempo marking of 152 beats per minute indicates that the basic quarter-note beat, found in the bottom number "4" of the time signature, will happen 152 times every minute.*

*A **metronome** is a useful tool in determining the pace of a musical composition. This apparatus produces a clicking sound whose tempo can be varied. Mechanical and electronic metronomes can be purchased at most music stores or can be downloaded as an app on the internet and run on a smart phone.

In identifying the tempo, you need only to find the basic beat as shown in the time signature and realize that the note indicated happens as many times per minute as the number indicated.

General tempo can also be described by a word or phrase (typically in Italian for classical music), such as **_Allegro_** (fast), **_Largo_** (slow), etc.

Tempo Markings Guide

Italian	beats per minute
Largo	40–60
Larghetto	61–65
Adagio	66–76
Andante	77–108
Moderato	109–120
Allegro	121–168
Presto	169–200
Prestisso	201–208

RHYTHM AND PITCH

As mentioned earlier, rhythm and pitch are the two basic elements of music. Pitch describes the frequency of a note (how high or low the sound) and is indicated by the vertical position of the note head on a staff of music. Rhythm, unlike pitch, has to do with time. It is the note and rest values (whole note/rest, quarter note/rest, etc.) that together work to form what is called rhythm.

READING MUSIC

Although music is an art form that a person can learn to do by ear alone, learning to read pitches and rhythms gives the musician another tool by which he or she can perform music.

To begin to read music, you must recognize written notes and know their location on your instrument.* You also need to have a system or strategy for counting out rhythms.

Although there are many possible time signatures or meters, this book concentrates only on the following four:

$$\frac{2}{4} \quad \frac{4}{4} \quad \frac{3}{4} \quad \frac{6}{8}$$

*The note names and their positions for the guitarrón are found in the photos, charts, and diagrams beginning on page 56 in this book and should be referenced as needed.

Below are some examples of a common and proven method of counting the rhythms in this book. Between each number count, the word "and" or its symbol (&) is written to indicate notes that happen between the numbers or beats.

Note: the use of a metronome is an effective tool in helping to maintain a steady beat while practicing.

a)

b)

In the following examples, notice the dot after the half notes; these notes are called **dotted half notes**. A **dot** placed after any note means that you add half the value of the note to itself.

c)

d)

In this case, we would take half the value of the half note, which is one beat, and add it to the half note for a total value of three counts.

A dot can be added to any note (dotted eighth note, dotted quarter note, etc.) and thereby increase its value by the formula indicated above.

Also notice that notes can be beamed or grouped together in different ways as is the case with Examples c and d, resulting in no change to the rhythmic value of the notes.

Example e shows a curved line or **tie** connecting the two dotted quarter notes in the first bar. The tie joins or combines the value of the notes. In this situation, two dotted quarter notes are combined for a total of six eighth-note beats.

e)

KEYS AND KEY SIGNATURES

With few exceptions, a music composition has a **tonal center** or **tonic**. Along with the mode of the music (major or minor, for example), musicians typically refer to this tonal center as the **key** of the music. To indicate the key of a piece of music, a **key signature** is placed at the beginning of a staff and is noted as a group of sharp (♯) or flat (♭) symbols. The **sharp** raises the pitch of a note by a half step, while the **flat** lowers the note by a half step. The notes referenced in the key signature (via sharps or flats) are used for the entire music composition, unless otherwise indicated.

As an example, the tonic (based on the key signature in a major key) and the pattern of sharp and flat placement on the staff (key signature) are illustrated below for several keys.

Tonic (major key)

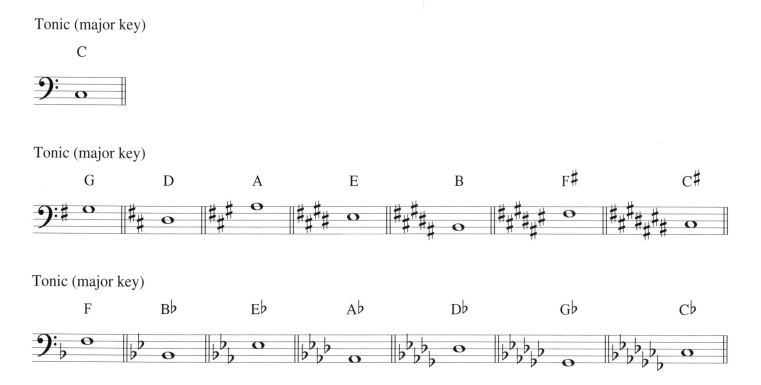

The information on the previous pages is intended to serve solely as a starting point in the understanding of music theory. The serious student of music is encouraged to seek out as many sources (books, audio recordings, musicians, teachers, etc.) to further his or her understanding of the art form that is music.

NOTE AND HAND/FINGER POSITION REFERENCE

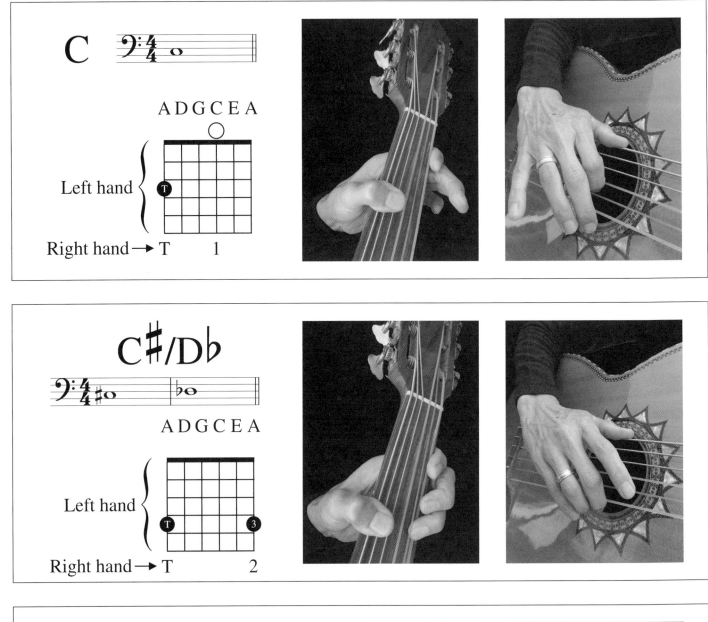

C

A D G C E A

Left hand

Right hand → T   1

C♯/D♭

A D G C E A

Left hand

Right hand → T   2

D

A D G C E A

Left hand

Right hand →   T   1

D♯/E♭

ADGCEA

Left hand

Right hand → T   1

E

ADGCEA

Left hand

Right hand → T   1

F

ADGCEA

Left hand

Right hand → T   1

F♯/G♭

ADGCEA

Left hand

Right hand → T   1

G

ADGCEA

Left hand

Right hand → T   1

G♯/A♭

ADGCEA

Left hand

Right hand → T

A

A D G C E A

Left hand {

Right hand → T   2

A♯/B♭

A D G C E A

Left hand {

Right hand → T   2

B

A D G C E A

Left hand {

Right hand → T   2

ABOUT THE AUTHOR

Herman Méndez received his Bachelor of Music degree with a focus on instrumental music. He enjoys performing and teaching an eclectic mix of music with audiences and students. As a public school educator, Herman has been (and continues in retirement to be) an avid ambassador for the arts.

Learn To Play Today
with folk music instruction
from Hal Leonard

 **Hal Leonard Banjo Method – Second Edition**

Authored by Mac Robertson, Robbie Clement & Will Schmid. This innovative method teaches 5-string, bluegrass style. The method consists of two instruction books and two cross-referenced supplement books that offer the beginner a carefully-paced and interest-keeping approach to the bluegrass style.

00699500 Book 1 Only......................$7.99
00695101 Book 1 with Online Audio..............$16.99
00699502 Book 2 Only......................$7.99
00696056 Book 2 with CD..................$16.9

 **Hal Leonard Brazilian Guitar Method**

by Carlos Arana

This book uses popular Brazilian songs to teach you the basics of the Brazilian guitar style and technique. Learn to play in the styles of Joao Gilberto, Luiz Bonfá, Baden Powell, Dino Sete Cordas, Joao Basco, and many others! Includes 33 demonstration tracks.
00697415 Book/Online Audio..........................$14.99

 **Hal Leonard Chinese Pipa Method**

by Gao Hong

This easy-to-use book serves as an introduction to the Chinese pipa and its techniques. Lessons include: tuning • Western & Chinese notation basics • left and right hand techniques • positions • tremolo • bending • vibrato and overtones • classical pipa repertoire • popular Chinese folk tunes • and more!
00121398 Book/Online Video $19.99

 **Hal Leonard Dulcimer Method – Second Edition**

by Neal Hellman

A beginning method for the Appalachian dulcimer with a unique new approach to solo melody and chord playing. Includes tuning, modes and many beautiful folk songs all demonstrated on the audio accompaniment. Music and tablature.
00699289 Book..................................$10.99
00697230 Book/Online Audio..........................$16.99

 **Hal Leonard Flamenco Guitar Method**

by Hugh Burns

Traditional Spanish flamenco song forms and classical pieces are used to teach you the basics of the style and technique in this book. Lessons cover: strumming, picking and percussive techniques • arpeggios • improvisation • fingernail tips • capos • and much more. Includes flamenco history and a glossary.
00697363 Book/Online Audio..........................$15.99

 **Hal Leonard Irish Bouzouki Method**

by Roger Landes

This comprehensive method focuses on teaching the basics of the instrument as well as accompaniment techniques for a variety of Irish song forms. It covers: playing position • tuning • picking & strumming patterns • learning the fretboard • accompaniment styles • double jigs, slip jigs & reels • drones • counterpoint • arpeggios • playing with a capo • traditional Irish songs • and more.
00696348 Book/Online Audio..........................$10.99

 **Hal Leonard Mandolin Method – Second Edition**

Noted mandolinist and teacher Rich Del Grosso has authored this excellent mandolin method that features great playable tunes in several styles (bluegrass, country, folk, blues) in standard music notation and tablature. The audio features play-along duets.
00699296 Book....................................$7.99
00695102 Book/Online Audio..........................$15.99

 **Hal Leonard Oud Method**

by John Bilezikjian

This book teaches the fundamentals of standard Western music notation in the context of oud playing. It also covers: types of ouds, tuning the oud, playing position, how to string the oud, scales, chords, arpeggios, tremolo technique, studies and exercises, songs and rhythms from Armenia and the Middle East, and 25 audio tracks for demonstration and play along.
00695836 Book/Online Audio..........................$12.99

 **Hal Leonard Sitar Method**

by Josh Feinberg

This beginner's guide serves as an introduction to sitar and its technique, as well as the practice, theory, and history of raga music. Lessons include: tuning • postures • right- and left-hand technique • Indian notation • raga forms; melodic patterns • bending strings • hammer-ons, pull-offs, and slides • changing strings • and more!
00696613 Book/Online Audio..........................$14.99
00198245 Book/Online Media..........................$19.99

 **Hal Leonard Ukulele Method**

by Lil' Rev

This comprehensive and easy-to-use beginner's guide by acclaimed performer and uke master Lil' Rev includes many fun songs of different styles to learn and play. Includes: types of ukuleles, tuning, music reading, melody playing, chords, strumming, scales, tremolo, music notation and tablature, a variety of music styles, ukulele history and much more.
00695847 Book 1 Only......................$6.99
00695832 Book 1 with Online Audio..............$10.99
00695948 Book 2 Only......................$6.99
00695949 Book 2 with Online Audio..............$10.99

STRUM SENSATIONAL SPANISH SONGS WITH
LATIN MUSIC SONGBOOKS FOR GUITAR
FROM HAL LEONARD

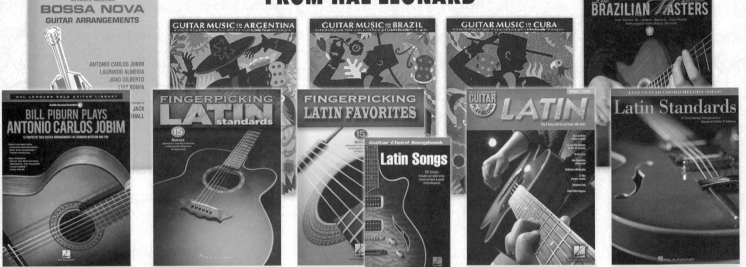

AUTHENTIC BRAZILIAN
BOSSA NOVA GUITAR ARRANGEMENTS
arr. Jack Marshall
20 solos from Bossa Nova greats Antonio Carlos Jobim, Laurindo Almeida, Joao Gilberto and Luiz Bonfa. Includes: Corcovado • The Girl from Ipanema • Insensatez • Journey to Recife • One Note Samba • Sambalero • Tristeza Em Mim • and more.
00123485.. $10.99

THE BRAZILIAN MASTERS
16 sambas and bossa novas by the genre's greatest composers. Songs appear in order of difficulty, allowing the player to improve their technique, musical expression, and understanding of this wonderful music. Songs include: Desafinado • Ebony Samba • Samba Triste • Little Boat • Sambalamento • So Nice • Solidao • and more. Also includes playing tips.
00378821.. $10.99

FINGERPICKING
LATIN FAVORITES
INCLUDES TAB
15 beloved Latin favorites carefully arranged to combine melody and harmony in one intermediate fingerpicking arrangement with tab. Songs: Amor • Bésame Mucho • A Day in the Life of a Fool (Manha De Carnaval) • Frenesí • Granada • How Insensitive (Insensatez) • Meditation (Meditacao) • Samba De Orfeu • Sway (Quien Sera) • Wave • and more.
00699842 Solo Guitar $12.99

FINGERPICKING
LATIN STANDARDS
INCLUDES TAB
15 carefully arranged, intermediate-level solos with melody and harmony combined for rich and satisfying performance material. Includes: Aquellos Ojos Verdes (Green Eyes) • Desafinado (Off Key) • The Girl from Ipanema (Garôta De Ipanema) • Quiet Nights of Quiet Stars (Corcovado) • So Nice (Summer Samba) • Triste • Watch What Happens • and more.
00699837.. $14.99

THE GUITAR MUSIC OF ARGENTINA
INCLUDES TAB
ed. John Zaradin
Popular Argentinean music edited and arranged for solo guitar. Suitable for intermediate guitarists and arranged in standard and guitar tab notation. Includes: El Cuando • Derecho Viejo • La Firmeza • Gato • El Maroto • El Palito • and more.
14013511.. $19.95

THE GUITAR MUSIC OF BRAZIL
INCLUDES TAB
ed. John Zaradin
A collection of 16 popular Brazilian music edited and arranged in standard and guitar tab notation with chord symbols. Songs: Baia • Corcovado • Desafinado • Garota de Ipanema • Meditacao • Samba de Una Nota • So Danca Samba • and more. Suitable for intermediate guitarists.
14013512.. $15.95

THE GUITAR MUSIC OF CUBA
INCLUDES TAB
ed. John Zaradin
A collection of 13 popular Cuban music edited and arranged for solo guitar. Suitable for intermediate guitarists and arranged in standard and guitar tab notation with chord symbols. Includes: Frenesi • Habanera • La Comparsa • Malaguena • Solamente Una Vez • The Peanut Vendor • and more.
14013513.. $19.95

BILL PIBURN PLAYS
ANTONIO CARLOS JOBIM
INCLUDES TAB
Hal Leonard Solo Guitar Library Series
This collection features fantastic solo guitar arrangements in standard notes and tab for 12 Antonio Carlos Jobim classics: Água De Beber (Water to Drink) • Chega De Saudade (No More Blues) • Desafinado • The Girl from Ipanema (Garôta De Ipanema) • How Insensitive (Insensatez) • Meditation (Meditacao) • Quiet Nights of Quiet Stars (Corcovado) • Triste • Wave • and more.
00703006 Book/Online Audio $17.99

LATIN – GUITAR PLAY-ALONG
INCLUDES TAB
Volume 105
The Guitar Play-Along Series helps you play your favorite songs quickly and easily! Just follow the tab, listen to the CD to hear how the guitar should sound, and then play along using the separate backing tracks. Songs: Água De Beber (Water to Drink) • The Girl from Ipanema (Garôta De Ipanema) • Ho-Ba-La-La • How Insensitive (Insensatez) • Meditation (Meditacao) • So Nice (Summer Samba) • Telephone Song • Watch What Happens.
00700939 Book/CD Pack.......................... $16.99

LATIN SONGS – GUITAR CHORD SONGBOOK
Lyrics, chord symbols and guitar chord diagrams for 58 Latin standards: Adios • Always in My Heart • Bésame Mucho • Blame It on the Bossa Nova • Brazil • Dindi • Frenesí • The Girl from Ipanema • The Look of Love • More • Say "Si, Si" • Slightly Out of Tune (Desafinado) • So Nice (Summer Samba) • Wave • and more!
00700973.. $14.99

LATIN STANDARDS
INCLUDES TAB
Jazz Guitar Chord Melody Solos
Chord melody arrangements of 27 Latin favorites in standard notation and tab. Includes: Água De Beber (Water to Drink) • Desafinado • The Girl from Ipanema • How Insensitive (Insensatez) • Little Boat • Meditation • One Note Samba (Samba De Uma Nota So) • Poinciana • Quiet Nights of Quiet Stars • Samba De Orfeu • So Nice (Summer Samba) • Wave • and more.
00699754.. $14.99

Order today from your favorite music retailer at
halleonard.com

Prices, contents and availability subject to change without notice.

0